Calling Time on Women's Wasted Potential

Mary Alys

Calling Time on Women's Wasted Potential

ISBN: 978-1-907540-88-2

Printed and Published in Great Britain by AnchorPrint Group Ltd

First Published and Printed: May 2013
Reprinted: February 2015

Dedicated to Lorraine who supported me in writing this book and all those women over the years whose conversations I found so enlightening.

Sadly Mary Alys passed away days before this book was first printed.

1953 - 2013

Calling Time on Women's Wasted Potential

Contents

Preface   1

Introduction   5

Part One – How did we get here?   9

Part Two – What's getting in the way?   25

Part Three – Possible solutions   45

Part Four – Resources   55

Books and sources used   65

Calling Time on Women's Wasted Potential

Preface

Mary Alys was a feminist and adult educator. A lifetime
believer in the power of learning to transform people's
lives. "Knowledge is power" it has often been said but
knowledge alone is not enough. People need the time and
tools to use that knowledge to the best of their ability for
the benefit of themselves and the wider community. To this
end, Mary devoted most of her working life to enabling
learners to gain those tools. Her experience of nearly 40
years comprised adult and community learning and further
education including women's studies, Access courses as
well as devising and managing innovative adult learning
programmes and English for Speakers of Other Languages
(ESOL) provision.

For over a decade, she led the way for the TUC in the
Midlands Region on the strategic development of the Trade
Union learning agenda to support the development of
union learning reps, a trade union intermediary who works
to enable colleagues at work to maximise their potential
through learning.

Mary was involved in a voluntary capacity with a number of change organisations most prominently, for 30 years, with the Women's International League for Peace and Freedom, the oldest women's peace organisation in the world looking at the root causes of conflict. She served on its International Board and acted as a UK Vice President. This work brought her together with women from over forty countries to hear and discuss the common issues that women share influencing the Organisation's work at the United Nations where it has consultative status.

Elsewhere in her personal life she always actively encouraged and supported people to develop their true potential. Her particular passion for women fulfilling their potential stemmed back to a period of teaching at a high school in North Solomons Province, Papua New Guinea in the 1970s where she realised that girls subordinated their potential in favour of boys' self-esteem. On returning home and after the birth of her sons, she explored this further and became more involved in women's politics, took up women's studies and completed a Masters degree in History with a feminist focus. She used this knowledge to run women's studies sessions at her local unemployed centre and in subsequent adult education. The need for women to have 'space' to think about issues and feel confident about expressing their views alongside many politically opinionated men was all too obvious.

Times haven't changed that much since then, even though it was more than three decades ago. The need is still there.

In the meantime, the workplace has opened up much more to women in terms of types and level of job accessible but the challenge remains as to how best women can truly access these opportunities and feel fulfilled. This is essentially the dilemma that this book seeks to explore.

Introduction

Women make up nearly half Britain's workforce and are excelling in education at all levels. Many families rely on women's income. However, women's skills are often underused with too many women doing jobs below their capabilities and others unable to access the training and learning to develop their skills, enabling them to fulfil their potential. They face multiple barriers preventing them from using their skills effectively whether that's due to caring responsibilities and lack of flexible working arrangements, occupational segregation or straight forward discrimination.

With women working below their skill level and often in low-paid, low-skilled, part time work, the UK is missing out on talent and the Women and Work Commission, in 2006, estimated that this skills gap was costing the country between £15 and £23 billion annually. Closing this gap could also reduce the pay and opportunity gap between men and women.

This book seeks to explore some of the reasons why so much of the talent and potential of women in Britain today is underused, not only to their own detriment but also that of the economy and society. I have written it because I feel we have spent so much time pressing for short term initiatives that, of course, all operate within the 'status quo' and whilst alleviating the issues for some women, have not attempted to address the root causes I believe to be at the heart of the problem.

I start by looking at our past experience of work up to the present day as it is important to put where we find ourselves, today, in context. As you will discover, many of the ideas and assumptions that come into our daily lives all have their roots back in time and have been influencing women's decisions and choices.

During the course of writing this, I had the opportunity to talk to a number of women in a variety of jobs and this together with my experiences working with women over several decades has confirmed to me what is getting in the way for women and wasting their potential. So, Part Two explores this.

For many decades women have struggled to overcome barriers some of which have fallen only to re-emerge in recent years. Understanding these barriers does not solve the problem. We need to find solutions and make change to move to a fairer society and free up women's potential. Changes do take place as time goes on but they don't keep pace with women's aspirations.

Through writing this I want to put all this on the table for women and men to discuss and consider how we might all be part of the solution in making change. I make my own suggestions but the reader must make theirs and most importantly act on them. For this purpose there is a resource section which I hope will be useful.

My book is by no means a piece of academic research. Many have tackled this and although I have used their work as reference, my work is a reflection based on our common herstory, changing trends and life experiences of women I have talked to.

One

How did we get there?

Over the last hundred years women's roles in the workplace have changed considerably. There have been gains and setbacks over the decades as women sought to claim equality in the world of work. It is important to see our position today in the context of the last century and beyond, so as to better understand the way forward and the implications of further change on women's position at work.

Separation of home and work

If we went back to the 19th century we would see that the wide scale industrialisation had the effect of moving women's paid employment from the home. Prior to this, goods were often produced by men and women in their homes and adjacent workshops. The separation of home and workplace brought to the fore views on which activities women were suited for and which, if any, paid employment was suitable for her. It was then that the notion of the 'family wage' and the idea of a wife engaged in unpaid domestic activities became prevalent. Women's and men's roles at home and work became increasingly defined with the ideal of the man as 'breadwinner' and woman as 'housewife'. Although the harsh realities of life meant that single women continued to contribute to the family income through working and many married women did need to work if the husband was unable to earn a family wage.

As a result of work moving out of the home or workshop into factories, work was redefined. It now did not include domestic chores and the census of 1881 excluded women's household chores from the category of "productive work", classifying housewives as "unoccupied", paving the way for the affront felt by so many women right to the present time that their running of a home and caring for a family is undervalued. Until this redefinition, official records of male and female economic activity showed little difference but as the decades progressed women's participation in work was generally about 29% until the First World War.

The War came and with it the need for women to replace men which saw an enormous increase in women doing what had been considered "men's jobs". Unfortunately this had little effect longer term as women returned to the home once the war was over. In wartime women are seen as a reserve army of labour. Again the Second World War had the same effect with a dramatic exodus of women from the workplace once the war was over as women gave up jobs for 'our boys'.

Types of work women did

Whilst all this was going on the types of occupation that women worked in also underwent change. Women in the 19th and early 20th century were employed in so called "women's jobs" in service, the textiles trade, as teachers, nurses and shop assistants. Regional variations did exist, for example whilst women did not work in the coalfields of Northumberland and Durham they did in the Lancashire coalfields. Again in Lancashire they were employed in textiles whereas in Nottingham they were only employed as outworkers in the lace and hosiery trade. In Victorian times there had been strong moral outrage at women working almost naked so close to men underground in mines which led to women and children being moved out of these types of jobs. For women in rural areas, domestic service and fieldwork were the only two options until after the Second Word War with many moving to cities to take up domestic positions.

Once we move into the inter war years, with the growing importance of new industries such as light engineering and rayon manufacture, women start to be recruited in large numbers into this work mainly in London and the Southeast as well as the North West. A third of workers in the Rayon industry were women and 100% of the workforce producing light bulbs.

By the 1950s there had also been a shift from service and textiles to the clerical and typing sector. These regional variations continued after the Second World War and they reflect the opportunities available to women, the wages available to men and customs regarding women's labour.

The sexual division of labour

Regardless of occupation women were usually in the poorly paid, low status jobs. The concept of a 'woman's job' and a 'woman's rate' were regarded as the norm, even where women were engaged in the exact same process as men. The debates on equal pay began in the late 19th century. Low pay predictably made it very difficult for women to support themselves, let alone others.

In the late 19th century and first half of the 20th century women were poorly represented in trade union membership and only half as many women as men joined. It did vary from industry to industry. In textiles, for example, women were well organised and earned good wages compared to other industries. On the other hand women were often excluded from trade unions, for example, The Amalgamated Society of Engineers did not accept female members until 1943. There was a fear amongst men trade unionists that women would undercut their wages and so they generally had a policy of exclusion to keep women working only on so called "women's processes".

In those days this sexual division of labour was regarded as natural and women's take up of low-paid and low status jobs was considered a matter of individual choice. These ideas do sometimes continue to exist today and ignore any sex discrimination as a factor or the circumstances that women find themselves trapped in which need them to take such jobs. Many modern day theorists reject these ideas and highlight what is called a "dual labour market" where "primary workers" have a stable career and "secondary workers" who are often unskilled are seen as unstable.

During the first half of the 20th century skilled work began to be defined as that not done by women. When women did enter a trade in numbers, for example welding during the First World War, the pay was immediately reduced and the job status reduced. Skills then were socially constructed.

During the Second World War things were different. Women were given the rate for the job when they took up a formerly 'male' job although some employers avoided equal pay by saying that women needed male assistance on the machines or that it was in fact "women's work". This resulted in women's jobs in engineering becoming defined as unskilled.

Women were also excluded from training and apprenticeship programmes by employers and male trade unionists alike.

So, it is on this legacy of attitudes and patterns of male dominance that our more recent position in the workforce has been built. Attitudes to women and work were generally shared by all parties, including women, with State policies reinforcing them.

Impact of class and marriage on women's work

The idea of the male breadwinner with the wife at home was seen as an ideal in the late 19th and first half of 20th centuries and most married women did not go to work.

During the late 19th century most working class women went out to work in their early teens but once married the tendency began to stay at home to look after the family and other relatives. Information from censuses tells us that in the early 20th century only 1 in 10 married women were employed outside the house, mostly in service or in teams with their husbands, for example as a cook and butler team. This was much lower than it had been in most of the previous century. So, women's participation in the labour market was on the decline.

As the housewife model increased so too did the rise of women who struggled for rights to higher education and who wanted to work in medicine and other professions. However, women who had been able to take advantage of some secondary and possibly higher education also encountered discrimination through the marriage bar. Marriage bars were a practice adopted from the late 19th century restricting married women from employment in many professions, especially teaching and clerical jobs. The bar was widespread in teaching after 1923 and although removed in London after campaigning in 1935, continued to be practised elsewhere until much later. Similarly, the bar was only dropped in the Civil Service in 1946. In 1942 it was obviously government policy. Andrew Rosen highlights, in his work on the 'Transformation of British Life 1950-2000', The Beveridge Report which stated 'during marriage, most women will not be gainfully employed'. Ann Oakley in her book 'Housewife' cites that a married woman having to work was considered a "misfortune and a disgrace".

There are debates on whether this approach was due to the newly emerging thinking around maternity and work or simply to reserve paid work for single women who were deemed not have a breadwinner to 'keep' them. Whatever the reason, the marriage bar and attitudes surrounding it acted as a brake on women's potential.

Motherhood and work

The industrialisation of the 19th century, with its effect of moving women's paid employment from her home and redefining women's and men's roles at home and work, also impacted greatly on how women's roles were increasingly seen as primarily mothers. Ann Oakley wrote her study of housework, 'Housewife', in 1974 and examined the changes that took place with the separation of the family from the economy. A lot of emphasis came to be placed on the importance of a mother to her child and throughout the 20th century psychologists and sociologists explored the issue. These ideas peaked in the 1940s and 50s backed up by the work of eminent researchers. They had a lasting effect on how mothers came to be viewed and added weight to the new theory that women should be at home caring for their children because it was in both their best interests.

By the 1950s there was the expectation that a married woman would stay at home to look after children and children's needs for the first time in history were viewed as more important than anything else. At the same time, as we have discovered, men across all the classes had become less and less involved in the day to day lives of their children and their role was that of 'breadwinner'.

Changing attitudes

The 1950s ideal was soon to become unravelled. By the 1970s things were starting to change as a man's wage was not always enough to support a family and some women wanted to work as well as care for their children.

Insisting that a woman's role was exclusively that of housewife began to break down with the arrival of labour saving devices in the home. Much of the hard labour was eliminated from household chores, transforming women's lives. The notion of "Superwoman" appeared and although many women would have recognised this as something they had been doing for a long time as they sought to maintain their housewife and mother role with small amounts of part time work, the fact that it came into public usage played a part in changing attitudes about women going out to work.

By the 1980s the concept of a 'Career Woman' had taken hold as more and more women were working and the years out for childcare began to shorten. By the 90s the ideal of a full-time lifelong housewife had gone and women constituted half the British workforce.

So, women were continuously evolving and redefining their own roles but perhaps unsurprisingly this didn't keep pace with attitudes which meant that women have struggled against family and organisational expectations of them as they have tried to fulfil their aspirations, as well as their perceived obligations and maintain or at least move towards some potential economic independence.

The breakthrough Equal Pay Act came in 1970 but was not fully implemented until 1975. It permitted equal pay claims if the claimant was engaged in work of the same or broadly similar work. However, in the interim period, employers unfortunately 're-graded' jobs in discriminatory ways.

In 1984 the equal value amendment to the Equal Pay Act gave women the opportunity to lodge equal value claims with some successful 'wins'. However, as with all legislation, it only works if someone is using the legal process and enforcing it.

By the 1980s stereotypes around women's careers were beginning to break down. The 1980 'Women and Employment' survey showed that 90% of women were returning to work after childbirth even if not to their original job. Though as Dex, Scott and Joshi have shown, in their work on women and employment, this also highlighted downward occupational mobility, the longer the break, the greater this was.

The 80s was a period of enormous change and by 2001 the census showed much more equality of participation across occupational groups. As men lost jobs in the traditional industries in the 1980s, part time work expanded rapidly and many women were drawn back into employment. According to the British Social Attitude surveys in the 1990s, this increased participation by women in the labour market was mainly amongst women with children.

This trend continues and many more women were now entering higher education. Black and minority ethnic women, in particular, were gaining qualifications. In the first decade of the 21st century women were making up 45% of the work force, married and unmarried alike.

However, wages generally remain low in the female dominated sectors and the gender pay gap has stood at around 18% for full time and 40% for part time. The Fawcett Society coined the term "sticky floors" to describe women stuck at the bottom of the employment ladder. Women also experienced what is known as the "glass ceiling" i.e. not being able to make it into the most senior positions.

There has without a doubt been a shift in how women are seen in the workplace as the male breadwinner family concept has waned. However, women are still disproportionately in part time employment and still doing most of the unpaid care work and society often relies on them for voluntary and community roles. It would seem that whilst the nature of roles at work have changed for women, attitudes about who should be doing the family and caring role in home are slow to catch up.

Jacqueline Scott, who has examined attitudinal change from the 1980s to 2002, has found change in attitudes to women at work to have been slow, whereas in society in general there have been enormous changes.

The numbers marrying halved, those divorcing trebled, the numbers of children in families decreased with more single parents and more cohabiting couples. She says,

> There still remains considerable commitment to the tradition of gender role divide and a concern that maternal employment may compromise family and child well-being.

The concept of man as breadwinner and woman as mainly responsible for the family is not unsurprisingly rejected by more women than men. The notion of a dual earning family by the mid-90s was being supported by both men and women.

In 1989 28% of British Social Attitudes survey respondents agreed that it was a man's job to earn money and a woman's job to look after the family but by 2006 this was only 15%. That women should stay at home when the child was under school age, 64% agreed in 1989 with only 40% agreeing in 2006. These percentages also differed across classes with professional and management women least likely to agree but always with men showing more traditional attitudes than women. Whilst in recent decades we have moved from the male breadwinner model to a rise in dual earner families these changes, it seems, have not had much effect on the division of unpaid labour at home.

Susan Harkness, in her essay, 'The household division of labour: changes in families' allocation of paid and unpaid work', 2008, has highlighted that although there has been a fall in the total number of hours spent on housework during this time, there are clear gender divisions in unpaid work even when both partners work full time. When men and women both worked the same number of hours, men's contribution is just one third of the total. When roles are reversed in terms of work hours it does seem that men's contribution to house work does rise with the exception of men who do no paid work where their contribution is only one quarter of the total. She suggests that notions of 'identity' play an important part in this. Evidently, the higher the family income the greater the share of the housework done by men. Alarmingly the increase in house work hours associated with having children is almost done entirely by women.

The concept of male 'breadwinner' has invariably devalued women's contributions to work. Unpaid caring and voluntary work is increasingly entrenched a 'woman's domain' despite some change in attitudes and legislation.

Looking at our history over the last couple of centuries, we witness a deliberate engineering of women's position in the labour market. If women were required to carry out certain roles, they were allowed to, albeit at reduced wages as those jobs can be re-graded to 'women's work'.

What of the situation in the home? It would appear that women must settle for only a share of a man's rate for the job as well as most of the housework. It is this 'unfair' context that I ask readers to consider where we are today.

Two

What's getting in the way?

Looking at how we got to where we are and the current situation around women using their skills to progress at work, it would seem vital to tackle some of the issues and barriers facing women if the situation is to change. Throughout women's lives it seems that there are a series of challenges that get in their way.

Early years

Once a child is born their role is already being determined by the toys they are encouraged to play with, the clothes they wear, and the expectations of their parents' family and wider society. This continues as they grow up becoming more and more influenced by the media, commercial interests and school. From an early age children are surrounded and influenced by attitudes and expectations. For many girls the messages they get from society, particularly around body image, have a detrimental effect on their progress through their early formative years to adulthood.

Young girls are expected to wear pink or maybe purple, look pretty and play with dolls or toys of a domestic nature. They seem to be increasingly sexualised as adult women's clothes and styles are worn at younger and younger ages. The girl who wants to be active in play or play with so called boys' toys is often branded as a tomboy.

Influences in early girlhood are still pointing young women in the direction of motherhood, domestic chores and certain future occupations such as hairdressing and beauty, modelling, catering, child care and other caring roles. Views about what is suitable for a girl still persist from previous generations and some women testify that these are becoming more entrenched. Similarly, boys are presented with toys and activities that shape their aspirations. This surely has a detrimental effect on how children see each other and their roles as they grow together into adulthood.

In most of my conversations with women, they have identified early influences and attitudes as being responsible for their slow or unsatisfactory progress in their job choice and world of work.

So, if we are to make change it needs to start early within families and schools to counteract the influences and attitudes if we are to build a more equal society. The often suggested positive role models must also play a part in children's education. Without this shift in early years socialisation, progress is going to be extremely slow with women experiencing a poor deal.

Influences on girls

Government statistics show that girls have been doing very well at all stages of their education. However, they are not showing up later in sufficient numbers in the subjects of science and maths which are subjects boys have traditionally dominated. This aggravates further occupational segregation with fewer than possible young women moving into and through those related occupations, all vital for economic growth and those women being given adequate opportunity to reach their potential. If they do access those occupations, they don't necessarily stay. The question 'why?' must be posed. What puts them off? It can't be fully explained as purely a matter of choice. What influences a girl to make this decision? Surely her upbringing, schooling and influences around her have some part to play?

Careers and guidance at school by practitioners and teachers alike was the subject of criticism by the Women and Work Commission in their 2006 report 'Shaping a Fairer Future'. The Report highlighted lack of appropriate careers guidance or the absence of it to prepare girls and young women for a realistic view of the options available to them. It was also critical of the lack of information on pay differentials between occupations.

Similar complaints about careers advice or the lack of it certainly came out strong in my conversations with women. The TUC, in evidence given to the Government in 2011 on the subject of gender stereotyping of certain careers, recommended that,

Young women must be given information about the earning potential and promotion prospects of stereotypically feminine sectors such as the so-called "5 C's" (cleaning, catering, caring, cashiering and clerical).

Whilst individual practitioners may be working hard for change, this is obviously not on a wide-scale basis. Teachers and guidance workers bring their attitudes formulated by their own upbringing and influences into work every day. So-called 'good practice' is only as good as the people delivering it and if their own attitudes are not firmly behind the process or at odds, one must worry about it is true efficacy.

Employers too must shoulder their share of the blame. Is their workplace culture appropriate to ensure they attract, recruit and retain female workers? After all, why would you avoid using the talent of women unless you held deep seated 19th century attitudes?

It would be true to say that many girls go through the system without feeling that they have had a raw deal but it is only in later life when they look back that they might begin to question their early experiences and wonder about the choices or the path they were set upon. Some girls question this system from early on and try hard to follow what they believe is what they want to do. This can be difficult for them if the role is a non-traditional one for girls.

Parents and the wider family also influence the girl's choices at school, her aspirations and the work path she is led towards. Then, whilst girls are making decisions that will probably determine their future work and gaining the appropriate skills for it, boyfriends and babies are added to their agenda. Attitudes and expectations of boyfriends, partners and husbands all begin to be added into the mix.

Later, in this context, I look more at choices women make, and ponder some very worrying trends in the, arguably, loaded decisions young women seem to be making, especially in response to the widening opportunities of apprenticeships on offer to young people.

Whilst some of the traditional attitudes identified earlier in the book have definitely been changing there is still a long way to go. The 'Century Gap', identified by Harriet Harman in the 1990s, is still there as men struggle to keep up with women's expectations and progress. There are positive signs as identified in the research on attitudes but there are still stark facts which show how slow this has been, all highlighted in Part One under Changing Attitudes.

Women with children

Two thirds of women with dependent children are in employment. The age of the youngest child is a key factor and just over half these women have an under 5. (Office of National Statistics) A smaller proportion of lone mothers are in employment, again the age of the youngest child has an impact on the employment rate of lone mothers.

The recent recession and cuts have meant that more women are now not at work and at home probably taking back more of the domestic duties and childcare if they have been to some extent shared. The Fawcett Society, in April 2013 reported a 26 year high in women's unemployment, now standing at 1.12 million, with almost three times as many women than men having become 'long term' unemployed in the two and a half years since October 2010.

Where will all this lead? Will men's attitudes to domestic chores and childcare take a backward step just as it seems it was turning a corner?

In the list of barriers getting in the way of women's progress and regaining of skills for the workplace, child rearing is high with issues arising from maternity leave, men's sharing of maternity leave and the return to work and subsequent childcare arrangements required.

Pregnant women have already been highlighted as the most discriminated against group in the workplace by the Fawcett Society, for some years. In March 2013, they again urged government to address the issue. They claim that

"...even before the recession began, it was estimated that up to 30,000 women had lost their jobs due to pregnancy discrimination."

Although against the law, the attitude still exists among some employers that it is better not to employ a younger woman in case she becomes pregnant and they have to deal with a maternity situation.

Fawcett say that there has been no national research into what they term 'pregnancy discrimination' following the economic downturn but that all the indications are that it has increased significantly. They argue that in times of austerity, when employers cannot afford to take any perceived risks to profits and growing business, discrimination against women in the workplace is likely to rise as women, particularly of child bearing age, appear to be the riskier and less affordable choice for employers. (Fawcett 2013)

For women who do get appropriate maternity leave arrangements from their employers and days during maternity leave to keep in touch with work, it can still be very difficult on return to the workplace to juggle the competing demands. They may still feel that they may have missed out on opportunities in their absence and struggle to keep up with any arising due to their complicated childcare and work schedule.

It is of course at this point that women can fall into a part-time work trap. More than three quarters of all workers in part time jobs are women. Part time work can also bring with it low pay, low status and insecurity of employment, perhaps on zero hours contracts or home working. This is very likely to mean that women's skills are under-utilised. The Equalities Review concluded, in their final report 'Fairness and Freedom' in 2007, that their research revealed clearly that,

> ...there is one factor that above all leads to women's inequality in the labour market – becoming mothers.

Whilst it might suit women in the short term to juggle all the many demands of life, in the longer term it will have a negative effect on their progress in the workplace.

Women find themselves forced into the position of having to balance childcare costs with going to work. This can become even more complicated after the first child with differing arrangements for nurseries and school times for two or more children. It is therefore not surprising that women often make that so-called choice to not work at this stage of raising a family. Interestingly this is not a choice that men often have to face despite the fact that they are equally responsible for their family.

Unfortunately the notion of the male breadwinner still pervades and this is accepted as the status quo by many men and women alike. Where couples are both trying to take equal responsibility many very often come up against the conclusion that in fact the man is likely to be the higher earner. There are examples of families where the woman earns the most and the decision is taken that the man will stay at home to look after the children but this is uncommon as pay rates demonstrate.

"Childcare is widely recognised as the number one barrier to getting to work. Without the presence of quality and affordable childcare, a woman's capacity to maintain their desired level of engagement within the workforce is considered to be increasingly difficult despite an increase in paternity leave provisions." Women's National Commission response to Commission on Status of Women (CSW statement Feb 2011)

As many juggle nursery school times and children's activities alongside work and domestic chores, years go by quite quickly. As one woman testified, there isn't time to think about what you really need to be doing for your own future career and economic well-being. We cannot possibly underestimate this issue of women not having the time and space to consider what is best for them.

As women get into their 50s they sometimes become grandparents and with that now comes further demands on their time, often given willingly of course. Some grandmothers feel under pressure to put their own work interests behind that of a daughter so that she can go to work whilst they look after the grandchildren. As childcare constitutes quite a cost it is sometimes only possible for a woman to go to work if she can utilise free childcare offered by other family members.

We must also bear in mind the detrimental impact on older women's pensions given that, for many older women workers, a lifetime of relatively lower income may mean that they find themselves having to carry on working as long as they can to reduce their poverty levels as pensioners.

...and women without children?

Caring responsibilities can extend beyond children to caring for sick or elderly relatives. In a family there is the assumption that it will be the women that do the caring rather than the male members of the family.

We must also ask ourselves about women who choose not to have children. They too find themselves represented in the vast numbers of women in part time, low paid caring related work. Young women who find themselves leaving school with fewer qualifications than expected, successful women on career paths who find themselves needing to care for an infirmed parent because society deems them able to as they are perhaps not married or have their own children. Ask yourself how many of your women friends without children find themselves with these or other types of caring responsibilities. I have spoken to many such women who secretly resent their male family members for the unspoken higher status that society bestows them - that it isn't their job to take on these roles.

Impact of racism

In 2006 a TUC report on Black Women and Employment revealed that black and minority ethnic women are more likely to be unemployed or economically inactive than any other group in the labour market. It highlighted cultural stereotyping by employers that results in them having to take jobs at a lower skills level than they are qualified for and stated that even when they are in employment, black and minority ethnic women are disproportionately likely to be working in temporary jobs.

The Fairness and Freedom report in 2007 found that Pakistani, Bangladeshi and Black Caribbean women found it harder than their white counterparts to get a job or win promotion, and were more likely to be segregated in certain types of work despite having good qualifications. The report blamed these barriers, rather than perceived family or cultural resistance to women working.

All these issues obviously need much more exploration but it is clear to me that racism throughout society plays its part in squandering women's potential and talent.

Training

Women too have told me that although they do undertake training at work, it never goes anywhere in terms of their skills being put to better use at work.

A higher proportion of women than men currently do undertake training at work or adult education. However, this can be partially explained by women's employment in greater proportions in the public sector where access to training can be better.

Although this may be the case, Matilda Gosling, in her report for the City and Guilds Centre for Skills Development: 'Who Trains? A Picture of Companies Training Practice Across the UK' 2009, highlighted that improved access to training opportunities at work does not necessarily mean that women are recognised and rewarded in the same way as men for the skills they acquire. She says,

"The finding that employers do not recognise women sufficiently for the training they undertake on the job adds to the bleakness of a lack of recognition of prior education and training. The pay gap between men and women, for example, is immediate for graduates: female graduates in the UK are paid 15% less than male graduates when they begin work, and more than 30% by the time they are in their 50s. The presence of a pay gap at the beginning of people's working lives suggests that the commonly cited reason for the pay gap - women taking time off from the workplace to raise a family - is not the only cause."

Choice

As we think about what's getting in the way, we do need to tackle the thorny question of 'choice'. With hindsight it can be very easy to look back and decide you have made a choice about something. But what choice really is choice? This can apply to boys as well as girls, for example, the labour market in your place of birth may determine the type of job available to you. So, labour market and assumptions about what is suitable for your gender means that choices are to some extent not real choices. However, for women, there is an added assumption based on the notions that exist in society about women's assumed responsibilities around rearing of children and care of other family members which seems very rarely to present as a choice for boys. Which choices did the women and men make in your family?

It is apparent that women often think they have made a choice. Indeed many women I have spoken to say this but on closer analysis it would seem they are only making a choice based on constraints society has surrounded them with. For example, a woman may have a partner who is keen to share childcare responsibilities but if their employer is not operating family friendly work practices and the partner can earn more, the so-called choice becomes a forced choice if the family are going to survive economically.

Many women do actually make a real choice to look after their children and stall returning to work. Should we assume then that their partners have 'chosen' not to stay at home following the birth of their children? Do men make a choice, a real choice, to return to work? How does it work for women with same sex partners? How many layers do the choices women make have?

Women's work experience has, over time, been one of interruptions due to caring responsibilities, mainly part time, across a variety of workplaces but more often than not involving caring for or servicing others. It is worth reflecting on the fact that women often do jobs that replicate their domestic responsibilities or use their 'feminine' attributes where, for example, glamour or sexuality are part of the job. Many women actually choose work that is of a caring nature because they believe that they are naturally good at this. Some of the women I talked to, when asked, pinpointed this even back to some point in their childhood. This must surely raise questions on how girls are brought up and what might influence them to choose certain pathways. Additionally women talk about feeling the need to do jobs that make a difference and therefore take up public service type jobs, for example in health and social care or the voluntary or charity sector.

Ideology still plays a major role in determining women's participation in the workforce. It restricts opportunities, as we can see today for example, in the gender differences showing up in the recruitment of apprentices, with girls mainly taking up the traditional women's type jobs of caring, hairdressing and office work and boys dominating in engineering, construction and IT. Although IT, in historical terms, is only a recently emerging work area, it is interesting to note how this has become dominated by men despite its emergence in decades where women were beginning to assert their place in the workplace. Readers will also be interested to note that the apprenticeship areas dominated by boys are also those attracting the better pay. All very worrying. Is history repeating itself?

A word on 'higher responsibilities'

A common theme, emerging from the talks I had with women, was the perception of the responsibilities and worries connected with taking a higher level job. I do wish to challenge where this assumption might have come from. It is certainly true that many highly paid jobs are virtually 24/7 with a culture of working early and late but it is equally true that there are women out there in very low paid jobs, for example in school canteens and hospitals, going the extra mile most days to get in early to prepare meals because their paid hours aren't sufficient to get the work done or to stay past the end of their shift to complete a nursing task for a patient or their mounting paperwork. Surely they have equally taken their responsibilities home with them to worry about and impact on their lives and still getting little monetary compensation?

Whose skills are valued?

As highlighted earlier, when women's jobs became defined as generally unskilled, many men's jobs were those that were deemed skilled. Recalling that housework had earlier been excluded from the definition of 'productive work', it is therefore not surprising that it doesn't seem to have been thought of in terms of skilled. Hence a probable reason why so many women, on seeking work after a long period at home, do not believe they have gained skills. Sometimes they fail to see the transferable skills they bring with them from running a home such as budgeting, time management and organisational skills, not to mention the high level diplomacy skills required to deal with the challenges children throw up. This combined with lack of self-confidence, perhaps brought on by society's expectations of them, can all lead to women underestimating their capabilities at all levels.

So, it could be argued that 'skills' as a term has been socially constructed, with the earlier definitions of skilled and unskilled work and how women's work was viewed still having a detrimental and lasting impact on limiting women's potential. All this underpinned by decades of society not seeing women as equals and their contribution as valuable.

I n answer to the question 'what's getting in the way?' this section has concentrated on the main themes that come to the fore. Employer prejudice, deeply engrained attitudes in society re girls', boys', men and women's abilities and of differing types of women, perceptions or expectations of the likelihood of women taking time out to raise children, as well as women's own lack of confidence in demanding recognition. In other words, settling for less.

It is overwhelming and may leave the reader wondering where to start first but start we must. Too much has been written, too many policies dreamt up and several laws passed to give up now. It's attitudes that must change towards all women regardless of class, race, disability, age, those with or without children, their sexuality or cultural and religious background. Change is always slow but if we want change, we have to start somewhere.

Three

What might be the solutions?

The solutions put forward in this section are ideas, many of which have been discussed over and over again in preceding decades.

Policy and legislation, whilst welcome, has arguably failed to a large extent. What's needed is concrete action to change attitudes and challenge the status quo.

Progress on any of these solutions might go somewhere over time in creating a different culture which frees women up more to take the decisions about work that really are their decisions not just an empty choice. A number of them are policy matters which could be enacted by any forward thinking government. The harder ones to crack are those that arise from deep seated attitudes and beliefs about women's role and predictably will take much awareness raising amongst men and women if they are to be changed. Also, once you start thinking about the core problems, there will no doubt be many more solutions or practical ideas that will assist towards change.

So, this section is about change and I will outline a variety of actions which combined could affect change. Who is going to make that change? YOU ARE by influencing family, friends, work colleagues, campaign groups. This is too important to leave to somebody else to do it; we've waited too long already. It is vital to find time for discussion and create awareness if attitudes are to change in the long term.

What follows is a list of some solutions and suggestions and then it's over to you for your ideas.

1. Better sharing of domestic labour

As has been highlighted in previous chapters, the last few decades have seen some progress in men changing attitudes and taking on more domestic responsibilities including childcare. However, if these responsibilities are to be completely shared it means that men have to take on the responsibility and not see it as 'helping' or 'assisting'. They need to be able to act without requiring direction or supervision. Some men do already know this but how do we move to a position where taking on responsibilities comes to all men?

This must surely stem from the way boys are brought up so, inevitably, it's about the parenting and messages they get as a child. Again, we can't make the mistake of laying this at the door of mothers who are not the complete parenting picture. It is everyone's responsibility. Women too need to be able to shift from their own perceptions of their role.

Within domestic labour, childcare is cited as one of the biggest obstacles for women. We should ask ourselves 'why isn't this the case for men?' Childcare it seems is mainly seen as the woman's responsibility and therefore costs and problems associated with it are there for the woman to sort out, often presenting her with limited choices.

Where there are two parents, these costs and solutions need to be shared equally between parents. There can be employer initiatives, government programmes, improved work life balance practice at work and other initiatives to support this but fundamentally, until the basic attitude is changed, these measures are superficial and not affecting the sheer numbers of parents to enable the change.

> Within domestic labour, childcare is cited as one of the biggest obstacles for women. We should ask ourselves 'why isn't this the case for men?

My thoughts outlined above have major implications for children's education, girls' as well as boys'. They are the victims of assumptions about their roles that permeate society. If a child could grow up unfettered by stereotypes and roles, how much happier might they be? Society would be moving towards real equality in practice. We already know that many young people develop their self-esteem problems as they try to conform to expectations of them.

2. Challenge early influences on children

In Part Two, I looked at the negative impact of gender stereotyping in children's toys and media aimed at children. It all starts very early on and there are currently growing campaigns to challenge this, for example, Let Toys Be Toys (see Resources Section). It is in these early years that boys and girls receive messages about their futures, so this surely is an area that cannot afford to be overlooked.

Contemporary advancement in men's and boys' attitudes to further sharing of domestic responsibilities is being undermined and undone by societies urge to pigeonhole children. Toys should be suitable for all children and careful attention to messaging. Increasingly over the last two decades toys seem to have become much more gender specific again to the extent that children themselves will tell you what they can or cannot play with on the basis of whether it is a girl's or boy's toy. Clearly an array of people need to take some responsibility here: schools, nurseries, after school clubs, youth clubs, church groups, children's television, magazines and comics and immediate and extended family. So often parents try to do their best on toy choice for children only to have their efforts undermined by their children's peers and parents as well as the institutions that are supposedly there to nurture and educate our children.

3. Challenge gender stereotyping in careers education

I explored the role of careers advice in limiting choices for women and girls and I have already highlighted the work carried out by Margaret Prosser, Women and Work Commission, which made a strong recommendation to government in 2006 to improve careers advice the girls.

Tackling gender stereotyping in the education system is key to reducing occupational segregation and hence the gender pay gap and it should start from early years.

All the women I've spoken with over the years, all too easily pinpoint the messages or lack of message they received in teenage years about their future options. It was particularly shocking to hear that only in the last decade a young woman attending a much sought-after grammar school for girls recounted how her whole class was told that there was no point in them thinking they could be a top businesswoman because they would need to prioritise their future family and domestic responsibilities. This in a day and age when various initiatives abound to encourage women into business and the boardroom. Old-fashioned sexism is alive and well and needs to be challenged. Are the children you know getting good, appropriate careers advice? If not, complain!

4. Challenge double standards

There are rather a lot of double standards out there when it comes to male and female roles and I hope my previous sections illustrate where some of those have emanated from. Some obvious ones are:

- Men getting praise for cooking or household tasks whereas for women it's expected and taken for granted that they will do it.
- Men who do the school run often get kudos and praise, whilst for women, it's expected.
- Women with childcare issues are not usually seen in a positive light at work whilst men can be, but on the other hand the same can apply to men.

- Many women state they have to work twice as hard as a man to be valued at work. How much of this is an actual truth or how women are made to feel is open for discussion.
- The idea that women are a special interest group must be challenged. Women make up half the population of the world. We are not a special case or marginal group. We need to claim our equality, surely that's fair?

5. Women not settling for less

This is key but probably, for women, one of the hardest things to do. As we know, many women spend their lives just trying to keep their head above water as they juggle their responsibilities. For lots of us, life hurtles by and there never seems to be time to think things through and if you do, where do you start?

When talking to women, specifically about this book, most said they had simply not given their paths through work much thought, mainly because they were too busy getting through daily life and all the challenges that presents. It was humbling to hear how the women had appreciated being given the time to reflect on their circumstances.

As a matter for your consideration, one of my questions to women was whether they thought they could do the job of their manager and you won't be surprised to learn that most said yes. One woman, having taken some time with me to reflect on her work and lack of confidence, went out and applied for a new job with more responsibilities having been in the same role for some considerable time.

I know, that's just one woman but if this is the power of women finding space and time to think, let's get out there and create some! Women could set up informal groups to discuss and reflect on their shared experiences and draw encouragement from each other. Isn't it time women stopped settling for less?

There is no need to feel guilty or have regrets. Remember, this is a long-term challenge which we can try and enact each in our own way and perhaps much of this is about laying the ground work for future generations, for example, letting children know they do not have to accept how things have always been. Above all, remember it is your life and you do not have to fit in with other people's expectations of you if you don't want to.

So, over to you now for your ideas. You may want to refer to my Resources Section to help you but I feel sure you have the drive and determination to play your part in helping to Call Time on Women's Wasted Potential.

Use the space on the next page to jot down your ideas or make a plan about one or two things you might do differently in future to help tackle the issues. Action speaks louder than words and enough has been written now. We know what the problem is; let's start changing this for ourselves. Today!

I'm really concerned that things are getting in the way of women reaching their potential, so I'm going to...

Resources

What YOU can do next

1. Make space for women to talk

Perhaps you could get a small group of women friends together to make space to discuss the issues or just one friend over a coffee. These are some of the questions I used in my conversations with women which might help. You can use them as starters or decide your own. The key is taking the time out to talk:

1. Tell me about your current and past jobs

2. What's your previous learning experience (school/college/evening classes/through voluntary work/at work)?

3. Why did you do this learning? How much of it was your choice?

4. When you were younger, was there a particular job you wanted to do?

5. How much have your jobs been your choice or have they been what was possible?

6. Is there a job you'd really like to be doing now, if all was perfect and you could begin again?

7. What would help you do the job you'd like/prefer?

8. Have you ever had promotion at work? Or, done different jobs at the same level?

9. Do you feel you could perform at a different or higher level than you currently do if only there was an opportunity? Or, do you think you have the skills for a similar level job?

10. Do you think anything has got in the way of you taking a different or higher level job? If not, why might that be?

11. What advice would you give to a young woman today about getting on in the world of work?

12. Is there anything else getting in the way of you reaching your potential?

Start asking questions.

How about speaking with your child's teacher at a parent's evening to see what efforts they make to tackle gender stereotyping in the classroom or ask them about careers guidance.

Perhaps you could go for a coffee with a friend and call into the local toy shop to ask what they can do to help challenge stereotyping of children's toys. Do they arrange them into girls' and boys' or pink and blue?

Can you encourage your women friends by asking them about their aspirations?

Can you ask your male family members what their thoughts are about taking on the care of a parent/elderly relative?

Are you an aunt or uncle? Could you encourage your niece or nephew to explore non-traditional careers or apprenticeships?

What message is your child's school promoting about apprenticeships? Can you and a friend ask the head teacher to ensure that teenage girls and boys are offered opportunities to explore a range of options?

What's it like at work? Could you ask your Trade Union to support you in your efforts to ensure fairness and equality for women who wish to progress at work and for men who wish to undertake caring responsibilities?

A Couple of Definitions

Causes of the gender pay gap

The gender pay gap is caused by differences between men and women in:

_ the jobs they do – *occupational segregation* – "women's jobs" are under-valued;
_ length of work experience;
_ number of interruptions to work experience;
_ part-time employment experience;
_ qualifications and skills;
_ travel to work issues;
_ unobserved factors including discriminatory treatment of women at work.

Source: Shaping the Future, Women and Work Commission, 2006

Occupational Segregation

Refers to the situation where some jobs are more typically done by men or women or other groups, for example a minority ethnic group.

Some organisations to explore - there are so many out there but here are just a few

End Violence Against Women - This coalition of organisations and individuals campaign to end all forms of violence against women. They lobby the government to take a more strategic approach to ending violence against women, including making a commitment to work which aims to prevent violence against women. They challenge the wider cultural attitudes that tolerate and condone violence against women. Sadly something that gets in the way of a staggering number of women reaching their potential in the UK.

Equality and Human Rights Commission (EHRC) – an organisation with a statutory remit to promote and monitor human rights; and to protect, enforce and promote equality across the nine "protected" grounds - age, disability, gender, race, religion and belief, pregnancy and maternity, marriage and civil partnership, sexual orientation and gender reassignment. The EHRC has a huge amount of free resources, advice and information for you to access. For example, there are specific lesson plans for challenging gender stereotyping in occupations, if you are a teacher.

Fawcett Society - UK campaigning organisation for women's equality and rights – at home, at work and in public life. Their founder campaigned for women's right to vote. Fawcett offer a lot of resources to help find out more about the issues and hear from other women who feel the same as you about fairness.

Gingerbread – a charity that works to promote the rights of single parents and does a lot of work to campaign for better public policies for single parents who want to work. They also offer training, have local groups and offer advice and information.

Let Toys be Toys – is a campaign group asking retailers to stop limiting children's imaginations and interests by promoting some toys as only suitable for girls, and others only for boys. They say toys are for fun, for learning, for stoking imagination and encouraging creativity. Children should feel free to play with the toys that most interest them. They say that it's time that shops stopped limiting our children's imagination by telling them that some toys are only suitable for either girls or boys.

Maternity Action an organisation that works to end inequality and promote the health and well-being of all pregnant women, their partners and children from before conception through to the child's early years. It claims that 30,000 women every year lose their jobs as a result of becoming pregnant and convenes the 'Alliance Against Pregnancy Discrimination'.

Pinkstinks is a campaign that targets the products, media and marketing that prescribe heavily stereotyped and limiting roles to young girls. They believe that all children – girls and boys - are affected by the 'pinkification' of girlhood. Their aim is to challenge and reverse this growing trend. They also promote media literacy, self-esteem, positive body image and female role models for children.

Trade Union Congress (TUC) - The TUC is an organisation with 54 affiliated trade unions, representing 6.2 million working people from all walks of life. They campaign for workers' rights and on social justice issues at home and abroad. They support trade unions with a wide range of resources to help tackle discrimination and have produced a number of publications specifically aimed at promoting women's rights at work. You could contact the TUC or ask your own trade union to find out more.

WISE (Women In Science and Engineering) – organisation that helps organisations to inspire women and girls to pursue science, technology, engineering and mathematics (STEM) as pathways to exciting and fulfilling careers. Their mission is to push the presence of female employees from 13% to 30% by 2020, boosting the talent pool to drive economic growth.

Women and Manual Trades – an organisation for tradeswomen and women training in the trades. WAMT has been championing tradeswomen for 30 years through campaigning and training, and says it's the only membership organisation specifically for tradeswomen.

Women Working in Construction (WWIC) – an organisation for all women who work in the construction sector and aims to raise the profile of women in the industry. It has an education remit too and works with school groups to demystify the sector and show young people that women are successful in the sector. They also encourage women to enter the industry if they are considering a career change or re-entering work after a period of absence.

Women's Engineering Society – similar organisation to those promoting women in other sectors but if you work in this sector, they are looking for role models to help them with their work in schools.

Websites

End Violence Against Women -
www.endviolenceagainstwomen.org.uk/

Equality and Human Rights Commission -
www.equalityhumanrights.com/

Fawcett Society - www.fawcettsociety.org.uk/

Gingerbread - www.gingerbread.org.uk/

Let Toys be Toys -
www.facebook.com/pages/Let-Toys-Be-Toys-For-Girls-and-Boys

Maternity Action - www.maternityaction.org.uk/

Pinkstinks - www.pinkstinks.org.uk/

TUC - www.tuc.org.uk/

WISE (Women in Science and Engineering) -
www.wisecampaign.org.uk/

Women's Engineering Society - www.wes.org.uk/

Women Working in Construction - www.wwicgroup.org/

Women and Manual Trades - www.wamt.org/

Social Media and spreading the message

Some Twitter suggestions here but make a note of your own to share with others.

Absurd Gendered Toys
@genderbiasedtoy

EverydaySexism
@EverydaySexism

Let Toys Be Toys
@LetToysBeToys

Pink Stinks
@PinkstinksUK

Over to you to explore but please join the 'Calling Time' community and share what you have done to Call Time on Women's Wasted Potential or to see what others think or to share examples. Follow us at @InfoCallingTime

You may wish to order further copies of this book. Any profits will be donated to The Mary Alys Trust which promotes the education of children and young people in conflict resolution, peace and social justice issues and taking into account the principles of feminism. Email: info@themaryalystrust.org.uk

Books and Sources Used

A Century of Women: The History of Women in Britain and the United States. *Rowbotham, Sheila.* Viking. The Penguin Group. London 1997.

Who Trains? A Picture of Companies Training Practice Across the UK. *Gosling, Matilda.* City and Guilds Centre for Skills Development. London. 2009.

Essay *Buffet, Warren.* Fortune Magazine.

http://money.cnn.com/2013/05/02/leadership/warren-buffett-women.pr.fortune/

Fairness and Freedom. Equalities Review Final Report.

http://webarchive.nationalarchives.gov.uk/20100807034701/
http://archive.cabinetoffice.gov.uk/equalitiesreview/upload/
assets/www.theequalitiesreview.org.uk/equality_review.pdf

Fawcett Society Briefing: Second Reading of the Children and Families Bill in the House of Commons.

http://www.fawcettsociety.org.uk/wp-content/uploads/2013/03/
Fawcett-Briefing-for-the-Second-Reading-of-the-Children-and-
Families-Bill.pdf

Housewife. *Oakley, Ann.* Penguin Books. London 1974.

7 Myths About Women and Work. *Fox, Catherine.* University of New South Wales Press Ltd. Sydney. 2012.

What about Women. *Fawcett Society* http://www.fawcettsociety.
org.uk/wp-content/uploads/2013/02/Fawcett-Society-What-
About-Women-report-low-res.pdf

Women and Employment. *Scott, J, Dex, S, Joshi, H* (Eds). Edward Elgar Publishing Ltd. Northampton. 2008.

Women in England 1870-1950: Sexual divisions & social change. *Lewis, Jane.* Wheatsheaf Books Ltd. Sussex. 1984.

Women in Work WIW 20. *Business, Innovation and Skills.* Session 2012-13. Written evidence submitted by TUC.
http://www.publications.parliament.uk/pa/cm201213/cmselect/cmbis/writev/womeninworkplace/m20.htm.

Working Women: TUC Education Workbook for all Trade Unionists. *TUC.* London. 1991 & 2005.

Shaping a Fairer Future. *Women and Work Commission* http://www.ukces.org.uk/assets/ukces/docs/publications/women-and-work-shaping-a-fairer-future.pdf

Social Trends 41 - Education and Training. *Office for National Statistics* Edition No: Social Trends 41 – 2011.

The Equal Pay Story: scenes from a turbulent history. Recording Women's Voices: TUC Equal Pay Archive: A filmed oral history. *TUC.* London. 2000.

The Century Gap: *Harman, Harriet.* Vermillion. London 1993.

The Glass Ceiling in the 21st Century: Understanding Barriers to Gender Equality. *Barreto, Manuela, Ryan, Michelle. K, Schmitt, Michael. T* (Eds). American Psychological Association. Washington. 2009.

The Transformation of British Life 1950-2000: A Social History. *Rosen, Andrew.* Manchester University Press. Manchester. 2003.